CAREERS IN CRIMINAL JUSTICE™

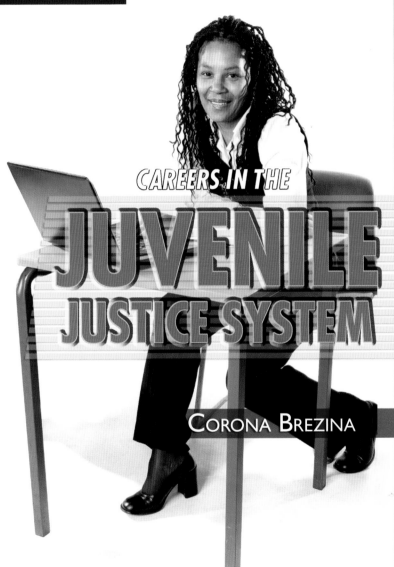

CAREERS IN THE JUVENILE JUSTICE SYSTEM

CORONA BREZINA

ROSEN
PUBLISHING®

New York

Published in 2010 by The Rosen Publishing Group, Inc.
29 East 21st Street, New York, NY 10010

Copyright © 2010 by The Rosen Publishing Group, Inc.

First Edition

Library of Congress Cataloging-in-Publication Data

Brezina, Corona.
Careers in the juvenile justice system / Corona Brezina.
    p. cm.—(Careers in criminal justice)
Includes bibliographical references and index.
ISBN-13: 978-1-4358-5267-9 (library binding)
1. Juvenile justice, Administration of—United States—Vocational guidance. I. Title.
HV9104.B74 2009
364.36023'73—dc22

                                                          2008046758

Manufactured in China

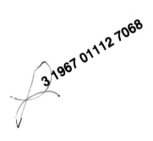

CONTENTS

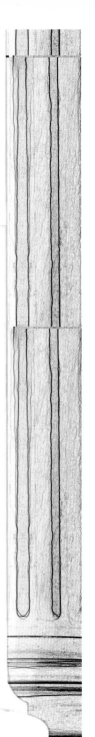

INTRODUCTION

Criminal justice is an exciting field with a broad range of potential career paths for job seekers interested in pursuing both highly challenging and immensely rewarding work. The criminal justice system is made up of agencies and departments charged with preventing and punishing crime. Within the criminal justice system, the juvenile justice system deals out justice to young offenders.

The first juvenile court in the United States was established in 1899. Reformers believed that juveniles should be rehabilitated, not tried and punished as adults. The separation between the two courts is based on the idea that young offenders are fundamentally different from adults. They lack adult maturity. They are more susceptible to peer pressure. Their characters are still being formed. Thus, they are not fully responsible for their behavior.

Today, most young offenders are still dealt with by a juvenile court that is separate from adult criminal court. The juvenile justice system offers the opportunity for intervention, rather than

Juvenile offenders in Texas are transferred to an evaluation and testing facility, where they will undergo psychological testing before receiving a final placement.

punishment. Most delinquent behavior has a root cause, such as family situations, mental illness, conflicts at school, substance abuse, or gang involvement. The juvenile justice system is designed to provide the means of changing an offender's attitude and behavior by addressing these underlying factors. Since the 1980s, though, trends have shifted toward harsher penalties for some serious or repeat offenders. Some teens are transferred to adult criminal court for trial instead of being dealt with through the juvenile justice system.

Juvenile justice is an ideal career choice for people who want to see justice served but also want to make a difference in children's lives. There are many different career paths in juvenile justice. Law enforcement officers, lawyers, judges, court staff, corrections officers, probation officers, counselors, educators, child welfare workers, and policy makers all have a stake in the juvenile justice system. Juvenile justice is a field that carries great responsibilities—it determines the future of many youth—but it also carries great rewards.

AN INTRODUCTION TO THE FIELD OF JUVENILE JUSTICE

Every day, the juvenile court system in the United States handles more than 4,000 cases of juvenile delinquency. An offender enters the system at the intake department, goes to court, receives a disposition (a sentence), and fulfills the terms of the disposition. The most common disposition is some form of probation.

According to juvenile court statistics compiled by the National Center for Juvenile Justice, courts handled about 1,660,700 juvenile delinquency cases in 2004 (the most recent year analyzed). The number of cases rose steadily beginning in 1960, peaked in 1997, then declined 10 percent between 1997 and 2004. In 2004, juveniles were adjudicated delinquent (found guilty) in two-thirds of the cases that went before the court.

The highest number of juvenile cases (613,200) fell into the category of property offenses, such as burglary, arson, vandalism, or trespassing. Despite this high number, rates of property offenses have fallen 29 percent since

Law enforcement officers may take a juvenile offender into custody. They also have the option of issuing a citation and releasing her.

1997. The next highest category, at 463,100 cases, was public order offenses, which includes criminal behavior like obstruction of justice, disorderly conduct, weapons offenses, and liquor law violations. Then, there were 395,700 person offense cases, such as criminal homicide (1,700 cases), rape, robbery, and assault. There were also 193,700 drug law violations. Fifty-seven percent of juvenile justice cases in 2004 involved those age fifteen or younger. Statistics concerning older teens are skewed because, in some states, adolescents over the age of sixteen are tried in adult criminal court.

On average, six out of ten juvenile justice cases are handled formally—the juvenile goes before a judge in court. The remaining four out of ten cases are handled informally, a practice usually called diversion. Person offenses was the juvenile crime category most likely to be handled formally, and serious offenses were more likely to be handled formally than lesser offenses in every category. Since 1985, the proportion of cases handled formally has been increasing. The number of cases handled formally grew by 80 percent, while the number of cases handled informally grew by only 15 percent. The largest relative increase in formally handled cases occurred in drug offense cases.

Although rates of juvenile crime have been falling since 1997, many people have complained that the juvenile justice system is ineffective because it is too lenient on offenders. This perceived crisis is due in part to the sensationalized coverage in the media of some high-profile cases, such as school massacres or extreme family violence. As a result, policies have shifted toward stiffer penalties that emphasize punishment, rather than rehabilitation. Generally, lesser offenders still receive sentences that emphasize rehabilitation, but serious, violent, and repeat offenders often receive harsher penalties. This might include a waiver to be tried in adult criminal court, mandatory sentencing, or a stint in juvenile detention.

THE JUVENILE JUSTICE SYSTEM

The juvenile justice system deals with young people who are detained for delinquent behavior. This means that if they had been adults and arrested for the same offense, then they would be considered criminals. Adults are dealt with in the criminal justice system. Young people are dealt with in the juvenile justice system. In addition to delinquents, the juvenile justice system also has jurisdiction over neglected and dependent children, children involved in custody settlements, special needs children, and any other juvenile involved in legal proceedings. (Dependent children are children whose parents are unable to care for them.)

The exact age range of a juvenile varies from one state to another. In most states, offenders under the age of eighteen are sent to juvenile, rather than adult, court. In other states, however, anyone under the age of sixteen is considered a juvenile. Some states also have an "age of responsibility," which ranges from six to ten. Anyone under this age is considered unable to understand the consequences of his or her actions.

Likewise, different states apply different definitions of delinquency. In addition to criminal acts, some states consider acts like truancy (skipping school), curfew violation, and liquor possession to be delinquency. The offenses in this category, called status offenses, are illegal only because of the offender's underage status.

Most young offenders enter the juvenile justice system when police or other law enforcement officials bring them in. Many large police departments have specialized juvenile crime units to deal with young offenders. The case may come to the attention of the police when the offenders are caught in the act or are reported by a victim or witness. In other cases, they may choose to turn themselves in. For very minor offenses, especially when the juvenile has no prior record, the officer may just issue a warning. For more serious offenses, the officer may issue a citation or take the offender to a juvenile detention facility.

If there have been formal measures taken against the offender, then the case will go to a court intake officer. The intake officer may choose to dismiss or divert the case. Diversion of the case means that the offender is dealt with informally without going before a court. For example, the offender might agree to a period of probation or community service.

Alternately, the intake officer may request a formal adjudication hearing—the juvenile justice system equivalent of a criminal trial—or recommend

A Coatesville, Pennsylvania, officer questions two sixteen-year-olds out past curfew. Both boys received a $100 fine for curfew violation, a status offense.

that the case be transferred to adult court. In some cases, the offender is held in short-term detention until the hearing. This may be for the good of the community, for the juvenile's own well-being, to allow for further testing and evaluation, or to make sure that the offender will attend the hearing. More often, the juvenile is released to a parent or guardian.

At the adjudication hearing, the offender goes before a judge. The proceedings are entered on the offender's court record. Many cases are uncontested, which means that the offender does not deny the charges. If this is the case, then the offender may enter a plea bargain in return for leniency.

If the allegations are found to be true, then the judge hands out the disposition in a separate disposition hearing, which is the equivalent to sentencing in adult court. Most often, the delinquent receives probation. The disposition may include fines, restitution (paying back victims), or community service. The offender may be referred to counseling for mental health or behavioral issues. For serious mental health disorders, he or she may be sent to a mental hospital. Some offenders may be conditionally freed but restricted by house arrest, electronic monitoring, attendance at a day treatment program, or other probation requirements. An offender may be placed in a foster home or other residential facility. The most serious offenders may be sent to facilities like state schools, boot camps, or other institutions.

Delinquents who have been through the juvenile justice system—in particular, those who have spent time in a juvenile institution—are released for aftercare, which is the equivalent of parole. If they are picked up again for another offense after they have been formally discharged, then the system will probably deal with them more harshly the next time around.

SPECIAL CONSIDERATIONS FOR JUVENILES

To some extent, the juvenile justice system runs parallel to the adult criminal justice system, but there are key differences. Many of these differences stem from the basic goals of the two systems. In general, the juvenile justice system aims to rehabilitate offenders, while the adult criminal justice system exists to punish offenders.

The difference between the systems begins with language. From intake to aftercare, the juvenile justice system involves specialized terminology that distinguishes it from the adult criminal justice system. Juveniles are not "arrested"; they are "taken into custody." Prosecutors do not charge them with a "crime"; they file a "petition" with the juvenile court. Offenders are not convicted and "found guilty"; they are "adjudicated delinquent." They do not go to "jail" or "prison"; they are "placed in an institution," such as a reform school or other state-operated juvenile facility.

Generally, a judge decides juvenile cases. Adult criminals have the constitutional right to trial by jury. Juvenile adjudication hearings are sometimes less formal than adult trials. The juvenile justice system was founded on the *parens patriae* principle. This is a "country as parent" philosophy, meaning that it is the duty of the government to act in the best interests of children who come before the court.

First-time young offenders in Greenville, North Carolina, can appear before a jury of their peers in teen court—a specialized diversion program—as an alternative to formal prosecution.

Although approaches to juvenile justice have in some ways evolved away from these roots, the juvenile court judge is still expected to approach the case from the viewpoint of a wise and concerned parent. Unless the charge is serious, the hearing may take the form of an inquiry, rather than a tense legal battle. Nonetheless, it follows the same basic procedure as

a criminal trial: presentation of evidence, testimony of witnesses, closing arguments by the prosecutor and defense lawyer, and so on. Unlike criminal trials, which are open to the public, proceedings in juvenile court are usually confidential.

The judge can take the offender's social history into account in choosing the disposition. This differs from adult criminal trials, in which the verdict rests only on the legal facts of the case. Before making a decision, the judge may consult a pre-disposition report on the juvenile offender prepared by a probation officer. Significant factors could include family life, history of abuse, psychiatric conditions, and prior juvenile record. Based on the facts of the case and these special considerations, the judge decides on an appropriate disposition. The judge has considerable leeway in imposing a disposition. In theory, the judge chooses a disposition that he or she believes would be most likely to rehabilitate the offender. Many states, however, have passed laws that lean toward punishing, rather than rehabilitating, juvenile offenders.

Juveniles can be tried for status offenses, which are not considered criminal behavior in adult court. In addition, the offender's parents can sometimes be held responsible for his or her behavior. For example, parents may be penalized for their child's truancy. Some states fine or jail adults who provide alcohol to minors subsequently involved in drunk driving accidents.

Despite the differences between the two justice systems, juveniles have many of the same rights as adults. Police must inform juveniles of their constitutional rights before an interrogation. This is known as the Miranda warning. Juveniles have

A juvenile offender restrained by leg shackles stands before the judge in a juvenile courtroom in Florida. Delinquents who are formally adjudicated establish an official juvenile court record.

certain rights during their trial—sometimes with limitations—such as the right to a lawyer and the right to protection against self-incrimination (granted by the Fifth Amendment of the U.S. Constitution) and double jeopardy (being tried twice for the same charge). Like adults accused of a crime, young offenders also must be proven guilty beyond a reasonable doubt in court.

PURSUING A CAREER IN JUVENILE JUSTICE

Working with the young offenders in the juvenile justice system can be both challenging and rewarding. A capable caseworker, an inspiring teacher, a passionate attorney, or any of the other professionals involved in juvenile justice can change a young person's life. Their work can open up a new future for juveniles involved in the system.

For a job seeker interested in pursuing a career in juvenile justice, there is a huge range of opportunities. Prosecutors, caseworkers, probation officers, corrections officers, and many of the other people involved in the administration of juvenile justice are directly employed by the court or by state or local agencies. There are also many community organizations and other groups that reach out to young people through prevention, intervention, and outreach efforts. In addition, juvenile justice policies and approaches are constantly being reevaluated

Roper v. Simmons

On March 1, 2005, the U.S. Supreme Court issued a landmark decision that abolished the death penalty for murderers who were under the age of eighteen when they committed the crime. The case centered upon Christopher Simmons, who was sentenced to death for murdering a woman in 1993 when he was seventeen. The Missouri Supreme Court ordered that his sentence be reduced to life in prison without parole because he was just a juvenile at the time of the crime. The Supreme Court upheld the ruling. This reversed a 1989 Supreme Court decision ruling that the execution of offenders who had been sixteen or seventeen at the time of their crime did not violate the Eighth Amendment of the U.S. Constitution, which prohibits cruel and unusual punishment. In the 2005 decision, the Court found that through "evolving standards of decency," American society and international consensus no longer condoned the death penalty for young offenders. Also, the justices took into consideration that juveniles are psychologically different from adults, stating that they are less mature and more vulnerable to peer pressure, and that their personalities are not yet fully formed.

Many key issues in the juvenile justice system have been decided through rulings by the U.S. Supreme Court.

and refined. Passionate individuals interested in revitalizing the system might choose to get involved in some of the innovative programs that feature new ideas about implementing juvenile justice.

A juvenile justice career is not for everyone. Anyone interested in the field must be enthusiastic about working with young people. He or she must be able to forge a connection with teens and children who may come from a difficult background, have substance abuse or psychological issues, or present other challenges. Juvenile justice workers must be able to work well with others. A single case can involve interaction with representatives from many different agencies and organizations, as well as with people from the youth's family, school, and community. Sometimes, the work can be frustrating or overwhelming.

Any job applicant is anxious to know the salary and benefits that come with the position. Pay for professionals in juvenile justice vary greatly, depending on factors like an individual's experience and education, his or her particular area of work, and whether he or she lives in a metropolitan or rural area. Juvenile justice job listings in the newspaper and on the Internet should give applicants an idea of the typical earnings for their geographical region and level of experience. In addition, national

Coordinator Keely Linton welcomes visitors at the grand opening of the North County Family Violence Prevention Center in San Diego, California.

statistics on wages for a variety of career areas are listed in the U.S. Bureau of Labor Statistics' Occupational Employment Statistics, which can be accessed online at http://www.bls.gov/oes.

2

CAREERS IN JUVENILE COURT

O nce a young person has been referred to the juvenile justice system and scheduled for an adjudication, he or she must prepare for a day in court. Every state has at least one juvenile court, sometimes called a family court or probate court. In large cities, the courtroom is part of a juvenile justice center. In less densely populated areas, juvenile hearings are held in the county courthouse.

Jurisdiction over juvenile justice cases varies from one state to the next. Many states have different juvenile courts for different categories of cases. One court might hear cases involving serious delinquency offenses, for example, while a different court hears cases involving status offenses. And still another hears custody disputes involving parents or guardians.

As might be expected, most of the people who work for the juvenile court have a background in law. The National Council of Juvenile and Family Court Judges recommends in its

Juvenile Delinquency Guidelines that court staff also be trained in "child and adolescent development principles, cultural differences, mental health, substance abuse, learning issues, and community systems and services." In addition, the court system requires administrators and other personnel to handle the management of the court.

GETTING YOUR LAW DEGREE

The path to becoming a lawyer requires hard work, academic excellence, and dedication. Ideally, it should also include a fairly clean record—candidates for the bar generally undergo a background check that will uncover any past criminal activities, arrest records, credit problems, or ethical violations.

A young adult who wants to be an attorney can begin preparing in high school by receiving a well-rounded education and maintaining good grades. Lawyers need strong public speaking, writing, research, problem solving, and analytical skills. Students can take classes or participate in extracurricular activities that will help them to develop these skills. High school students may also consider taking on summer jobs or doing volunteer work related to the legal system or public service.

A student must earn a bachelor's degree before attending law school. Although some colleges and

universities offer pre-law programs, law schools do not require any specific major. A student may choose a liberal arts major broadly applicable to law, such as philosophy or history. He or she may also choose a major applicable to a specialized field of law, such as economics or computer science. Even if the undergraduate major has no direct connection to law, what matters most is maintaining a good academic record. Law schools also require that applicants take the Law School Admission Test (LSAT).

Anybody considering law school should be enthusiastic about spending long hours studying. Competition for admission is intense—good grades and a high LSAT score will improve chances of admittance.

Once in law school, students choose a specific field of study. Those interested in juvenile justice should choose an area that is in some way relevant to the juvenile justice system. Areas of specialized study include family law, public interest law, and criminal law. In some law schools, students can enroll in a juvenile justice or family court clinic, where, under the supervision of clinic faculty and staff, they provide legal assistance to juveniles.

Law students generally complete their Juris Doctor (J.D.) degrees in three years. Before starting

Although juvenile court procedures are similar to those of adult criminal trials, prosecutors and defense attorneys are less adversarial and more cooperative in a juvenile courtroom.

to practice law, however, the graduate must take the state bar exam and a national ethics exam. Upon passing both of these, he or she receives a license from the state to practice law.

PROSECUTING ATTORNEY

Attorneys typically function as both advisers and advocates in legal matters. Advocates are people who argue on their clients' behalf and represent their best interests. They advise their clients by providing legal guidance and suggesting what steps to take in legal matters. They also act as their clients' advocate in court, representing their case before a judge. For prosecuting attorneys, their client is the government—on a federal, state, or local level—and they are employed to present the case against lawbreakers. Since juveniles are very rarely prosecuted in federal court, most are tried under state juvenile justice systems.

In adult criminal court, there is often an adversarial relationship between prosecuting and defense attorneys. Prosecutors want the defendant brought to justice, while defenders represent their client's interests. There is a different dynamic in juvenile court. Ideally, everybody involved in a juvenile justice case wants to bring about a disposition that is most beneficial for the juvenile.

Andrew Vachss

Andrew Vachss is one of America's best-known attorneys specializing in juvenile justice. Vachss represents children exclusively. He has also championed child protection legislation and served as director of the Juvenile Justice Planning Project in New York.

Vachss grew up in New York and received his law degree at the New England School of Law in Boston, Massachusetts. Before becoming an attorney, he was a federal investigator of sexually transmitted diseases, an aid worker in Africa, a labor organizer, and a prison director. Although the pursuit of justice for children is Vachss's life work, many people know him best as a writer. He has contributed many articles to *Parade* magazine and other publications, and he has written two textbooks on juvenile crime. He also writes fiction and is well-known for his gritty mystery series featuring an unconventional investigator named Burke. Much of Vachss's fiction draws attention to social issues, especially the plight of abused children.

One of the prosecutor's most important duties is that of gatekeeper, in a sense, to the courtroom. The prosecutor is one of the key figures in deciding whether or not a case should be given an adjudication hearing. Alternatives include diversion or transfer of the juvenile to adult criminal court. A prosecutor can file a waiver with the juvenile court judge requesting that the juvenile be transferred to adult court. In some states, the prosecutor can directly file the case to adult criminal court.

For cases that go to court, the prosecutor prepares a case against the juvenile and presents it before the judge. He or she introduces evidence, which can include physical evidence and witness testimony. The prosecutor examines the witnesses—asks questions— and then the defense attorney cross-examines the witnesses. The adjudication ends with the prosecution presenting closing arguments, followed by the defense attorney's closing arguments, and then a final rebuttal (response) by the prosecution. In some states, the prosecution also participates in the disposition hearing.

DEFENSE ATTORNEY

In 1967, the Supreme Court issued a ruling on the case of *In re Gault*, one of the landmark decisions concerning juvenile adjudication. Three years earlier, fifteen-year-old Gerald Gault had been taken into custody for making obscene phone calls to a neighbor. His parents were not informed of his detention and upcoming adjudication, and the neighbor never appeared to testify in court. Gault was found delinquent and committed to the state

reform school until the age of twenty-one. He appealed the case. Eventually, the Supreme Court overturned the conviction, ruling that juveniles facing institutional confinement—the juvenile justice system's equivalent of jail time—are entitled to certain constitutional rights, including the right to an attorney.

Juvenile justice defense lawyers represent their clients from the early stages, such as initial police interrogation, through the adjudication and

A juvenile offender in lockup meets with his attorney. Many delinquents who cannot afford to hire a lawyer are represented by court-appointed public defenders.

disposition hearing, and in any appeals. They advise their clients and, in some cases, may exercise the right to go forward with an adjudication, rather than settling for diversion or a plea bargain. At the adjudication, the defense attorney presents evidence that supports the client's case after the prosecution has rested. At the disposition hearing, the defense attorney may argue for a lighter disposition. The attorney may also attend subsequent court proceedings, such as reviews of plea

Teen Court

In most states, juvenile delinquents are not eligible for trial by jury. During the 1990s, however, some states adopted teen courts as a diversion option. Eligible teens—generally non-serious, first-time offenders—are dealt with by their peers. In most cases, the offender has already admitted to the offense. Rather than determining guilt or innocence, the teen court decides on a penalty.

There are four typical models for a teen court. In most teen courts, an adult serves as the judge while teens issue the disposition and take the roles of attorneys, jurors, and other court personnel. In the peer jury model, the case is put directly before a jury of teens. In the youth tribunal model, youth attorneys argue the offender's case before three youth judges. In the youth judge model, every role—including that of the judge—is filled by teens. No matter which model, adults administer the details of the disposition.

The use of teen courts is somewhat controversial. Advocates claim that offenders are likelier to heed warnings and penalties issued by their peers. They also say that every teen who plays a role in teen court benefits from the process. Critics claim that teen courts are a waste of resources. They say that offenses dealt with in teen court are so minor that they probably would not have been dealt with formally in juvenile court, and teen courts are an unnecessary supplement to the juvenile justice system.

agreement compliance or expungement hearings. At hearings on expungement of their juvenile record, delinquents who have met their obligations or have "aged out" of the juvenile justice system can ask to have their records sealed or erased.

Lawyers representing juveniles should be experienced in working with young offenders and be familiar with the procedures of the juvenile justice system (which do not always match up with those of the adult criminal justice system). Defense attorneys tend to take one of two approaches toward representing juvenile clients. They may take on a quasi–social worker role, in which they work with the prosecutor, probation officer, and other parties toward a solution that is in the client's best interest, even if the juvenile might consider it a punishment. On the other hand, they might vigorously defend the case and push for acquittal, much as they would represent an adult in criminal court.

Juveniles can hire a defense attorney on their own. If they cannot afford to do so, then the court will appoint a juvenile public defender to represent them. Some juvenile defender programs provide highly trained and motivated defense lawyers for offenders. But many juvenile public defenders carry huge caseloads and do not have access to adequate resources. In addition, they often lack specialized training in juvenile justice.

Chief family court judge Jerilyn L. Borack of Sacramento, California, signs court orders. Family court deals with cases such as divorce, child custody, and domestic violence.

JUVENILE COURT JUDGE

Juvenile court and family court judges are either elected or appointed to their positions. A judge must have a law degree, and most judges establish a distinguished background in their field of law before becoming a judge.

In the juvenile justice system, judges are responsible for far more than presiding over the

bench. They may be in charge of overseeing the budget, hiring personnel, and setting rules. They might personally supervise case scheduling and other administrative tasks. In very busy courts, they delegate some of these responsibilities to other court personnel.

The judge has the final authority over a juvenile's fate. If a prosecutor has requested a waiver to adult court, then the judge makes a decision on whether or not to grant it. In the courtroom, the judge maintains order and makes rulings on various issues—for example, if evidence is admissible—during the adjudication. At the end of the adjudication, he or she determines whether or not the juvenile has engaged in delinquent conduct. Before the disposition hearing, the judge meets with the probation officer assigned to the case to review additional information, such as the juvenile's social history, which is sometimes compiled in a pre-disposition report. At the disposition hearing, the judge hands down the final disposition.

Ideally, on top of legal knowledge, a juvenile court judge should be familiar with child and adolescent development, community and social welfare services in the area, and the appropriate rehabilitation measures for different scenarios. Some experts have advised that juvenile judges serve for two years, three years, six years, or even longer. In reality, though, many juvenile courts do not mandate any particular experience or training for judges. In some jurisdictions, judges are assigned to juvenile courts for just six months or a year.

OTHER POSITIONS

In addition to the lawyers and the judge, there are a number of personnel who handle the many aspects of the administration and organization of

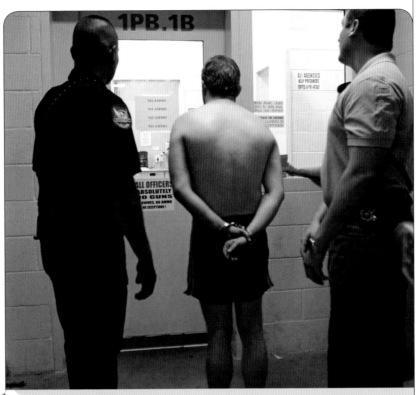

A police officer and a sheriff's deputy in Arizona wait in the pre-intake area with a suspect detained for a string of shootings.

the juvenile court. Some of the individuals who work with young people and their families are directly employed by the juvenile court. Others, such as specialists in various diversion programs or mental health professionals, work for social service agencies or other organizations.

The organization of the juvenile justice system varies from state to state. One state's juvenile court

Susan Hanson hands the results of a drug test to a coworker at the end of a weekly court proceeding. Hanson is program manager for Mental Health Systems Drug Court in Vista, California.

may have an assortment of directors, coordinators, executives, superintendents, managers, supervisors, and specialized officers that do not have exact equivalents in other states' courts. Instead of focusing on job titles, a job seeker in the field should look closely at the responsibilities and requirements for each position.

Most of these positions require a background in law, criminal justice, social work, or other relevant fields. For jobs that require working with juveniles,

the employer generally requires a background check. In some areas, being bilingual often gives the applicant an edge.

After a young person is referred to the juvenile justice system, he or she is screened in a process called intake, which is handled by the intake officer. Intake is not the same as "booking" a criminal. Instead, intake usually takes the form of a prescheduled conference with the juvenile and his or her parents. The intake officer decides whether or not the offender should be dismissed, diverted, or scheduled for an adjudication hearing. In most cases, the intake officer is a probation officer or prosecutor.

The juvenile court administrator manages the staff, budget, and policy for the juvenile court. He or she coordinates the activities of different departments, such as detention and probation, and acts as a liaison with other agencies and community programs. The juvenile court administrator may serve on boards and task forces that are related to juvenile justice. In some cases, the administrator monitors any research or grant work being conducted in the juvenile court. He or she oversees scheduling, addresses complaints, and resolves conflicts.

In some jurisdictions, juvenile court masters may conduct hearings. Juvenile court masters are lawyers, not judges, and are generally assigned cases that involve lesser offenses or formalities. In busy courts, they can relieve some of the juvenile court judge's workload. Alternate job titles for this type of position include judicial officer, magistrate, referee, hearing officer, and associate judge.

The juvenile court clerk, sometimes called a court case manager or legal administrative assistant, oversees the paperwork involved with the cases being heard in the courtroom. He or she compiles all of the relevant documents prior to the hearing. These might include affidavits, reports, and other files released by different departments and offices. The juvenile court clerk confirms that all of the parties involved in the case are present at the hearing and offers assistance before, during, and after the hearing. Following the hearing, the court clerk distributes copies of the judge's findings and orders. A clerk's specific duties outside of the courtroom vary from one court to another. They may include paralegal work, dealing with the public, and contacting juveniles and their families.

3

CAREERS IN PROBATION AND CORRECTIONS

When the juvenile court judge hands down the disposition—usually probation, sometimes confinement to an institution, and occasionally dismissal—the case moves from the hands of the court to the domain of the probation and corrections staff. These officers will monitor and participate in the juvenile's treatment as he or she fulfills the terms of the disposition.

A probation officer supervises a juvenile who receives a disposition of probation. He or she can either be an employee of the court or of a separate agency. A probation officer's job is part law enforcement and part social work. In *Juvenile Justice*, Rolando del Carmen describes how the probation officer is expected to be "a cop, a prosecutor, a confessor, a rat, a teacher, a friend, a problem solver, a crisis manager, a hand-holder, and a community resource specialist."

The Day Reporting Center in Sacramento, California, run by the County Probation Department, provides delinquent youth with education, vocational training, counseling, and recreational activities.

A small proportion of offenders receive a disposition of confinement to an institution. There are different types of juvenile corrections institutions, run publicly or privately, with varying personnel requirements. Corrections officers may staff such facilities, but alternate job titles include juvenile caseworker, detention officer, corrections counselor, and juvenile services officer, among others. Job seekers should read the requirements for the

The Juvenile Justice and Delinquency Prevention Act

The Juvenile Justice and Delinquency Prevention Act (JJDPA), which the U.S. Congress passed in 1974, set requirements for holding juveniles in custody. The first part of the act addresses status offenders and other non-delinquent youth, such as victims of parental neglect. The act states that these youths should not be held in secure facilities, since they are not delinquents. The second part of the act prohibits juveniles from being confined with adults. It established the "sight and sound separation" requirement, which means that juveniles and adults held in the facility should not be able to see or talk to each other.

The JJDPA is periodically revised and reauthorized by Congress. In 1980, the act was amended to prohibit juvenile delinquents from being detained or confined in adult jails or lockups. Another amendment, which was passed in 1992, addresses racial issues. States that have a large proportion of minority youths in custody must investigate and address the causes for such high rates of delinquency and incarceration. The bill introduced to Congress in 2008 placed an increased emphasis on mental health and drug treatment.

The terms of the JJDPA were not made mandatory. States that do not comply, however, risk losing federal money for projects, such as road construction or other programs.

position closely, rather than deciding whether or not to apply based on the job title alone.

PROBATION OFFICER

Probation is the most common disposition for juvenile delinquents. Most first-time offenders are put on probation, especially in cases of minor offenses or status offenses. Serious and repeat offenders often receive probation as well. Placement in a juvenile institution, such as a reform school, is generally reserved for the worst offenders. This is because juvenile institutions have been criticized on the grounds that the institutional environment is more likely to turn lesser offenders into criminals than it is to rehabilitate them. In addition, probation is far less expensive than confinement.

Although the common perception is that a probation officer's job is to oversee offenders who have received their disposition, the officer's role begins much earlier in the process. Probation officers often serve as intake officers. In this capacity, they can recommend diversion when they think it is appropriate.

The probation officer is also responsible for the pre-disposition report. This report describes the juvenile's family life, school history, work history (if any), prior involvement with the juvenile justice

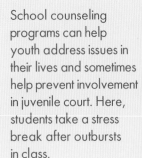

School counseling programs can help youth address issues in their lives and sometimes help prevent involvement in juvenile court. Here, students take a stress break after outbursts in class.

system, and any other pertinent information. The probation officer might consult school records, police files, and medical records. He or she may interview the juvenile's family, friends, teachers, police officers, and, when relevant, the victim. After evaluating the facts, the probation officer recommends a disposition to the judge.

During probation, the juvenile must meet specific terms that are intended to promote rehabilitation. The specific terms are left to the discretion of the

judge. They generally involve certain requirements (such as completing an anger management course or doing community service), along with certain restrictions (such as a curfew). Standard probation conditions include staying out of trouble, agreeing to drug testing, keeping in regular contact with the probation officer, and not associating with anyone who has a criminal record.

Probation practices vary from state to state, and probation officers are often on the cutting edge of new approaches to rehabilitation and experimental programs. In some places, serious or repeat offenders might be assigned intensive supervision probation. The probation officer closely monitors the juvenile, both at scheduled meetings and random spot checks. The probation officer also contacts family members, teachers, and other key players in the young offender's life. The offender may be restricted to home, except for approved activities, or he or she may be put under a rigid curfew.

Some states have instituted a practice of school-based probation. The probation officer has an office in a school, where he or she can easily monitor offenders and stay in contact with school administrators. The probation officer also serves as an ambassador of the juvenile justice system within the school and may implement prevention and awareness programs for the general student body.

In a practice called shock probation, the offender receives a disposition of confinement but is released to probation after a short period of detention in a juvenile facility. The period of confinement is intended to give the offender a strong warning and a vivid example of the consequences for criminal behavior.

The probation officer keeps the offender informed of any developments in his or her case and offers counseling and guidance. Probation officers also help offenders obtain services, such as

A probation officer talks to a girl confined to a juvenile center during a holiday party. The girl was feeling unhappy because her family could not visit her on Christmas.

counseling or drug treatment programs, and they may provide transportation in some instances. In addition, probation officers supervise aftercare—the juvenile justice equivalent of parole—when a juvenile is released from confinement. Aftercare is intended as a period of supervised readjustment into the community. Many of the conditions for aftercare are similar to probation conditions.

If an offender violates the conditions of probation, then probation can be revoked. When an offender commits a technical violation of probation, the probation officer must deal with the violation as he or she deems appropriate. A technical violation is non-delinquent behavior, such as failing to comply with a treatment plan, skipping a meeting with the probation officer, or failing to pay restitution. The probation officer will probably let the juvenile off with a warning for a few violations, but repeated violations will probably result in a revocation hearing. If the offender commits another delinquent act, then he or she may either be referred for a revocation hearing or sent back to the juvenile court for adjudication. As with the disposition hearing, the probation officer prepares a report that states the facts of the case and recommends a penalty. Options include harsher probation terms or commitment to an institution.

The responsibility for carrying out court orders falls to probation officers. These could involve performing searches, seizing evidence, or making arrests. A probation officer's job can be dangerous, and in some places, probation officers are permitted to carry firearms.

A probation officer must be knowledgeable in juvenile justice laws and procedures, as well as psychology and criminology. He or she must be able to work independently and must have exceptional problem-solving and organization skills. A probation officer might be required to exercise good judgment in stressful situations, such as a family crisis intervention.

Excellent oral and written communication skills are essential to a probation officer's work. The job will present situations that require a range of interpersonal skills: supervising and advising the juvenile; conferring with parents, lawyers, and social services personnel; participating in formal court hearings; and making presentations to community groups. Although being a probation officer is not a typical desk job, it does require careful attention to a great deal of paperwork. In addition to the pre-disposition report, the probation officer must manage and update each offender's files and performance reports.

Being a probation officer is a demanding job. Probation officers may find that they carry large caseloads but are not provided adequate resources to do their work. The job often requires extensive fieldwork and travel. Probation officers usually choose the field because they want to make a difference in the lives of young people, but they can become frustrated with these kinds of difficulties in carrying out their mission.

Most employers require that probation officers have a four-year degree in criminal justice, in a behavioral science like psychology or sociology, in social work, or in another relevant area. Young people who are just entering the job market can

The Missouri Model

In 2008, Missouri's Division of Youth Services (DYS) was recognized as a winner of the Annie E. Casey Innovations Award in Children and Family System Reform, awarded every year by Harvard University's Kennedy School of Government. The Missouri DYS emphasizes a therapeutic approach toward treatment, individualized assistance with education, and a strong family and community support system. Rather than being confined and supervised by guards, teens in Missouri's system participate in treatment programs administered by trained staff. Youths are housed in one of thirty-two small cottage- or dormitory-type residences. There are also day treatment options, which allow young offenders to continue living with their families while receiving treatment and paying their penalty.

Missouri's program has achieved measurable success. There is a low rate of violent crime or repeat offenses for graduates of DYS programs. The emphasis on education has also produced results. Most youths earn school credit during the program, and half return to school afterward. Most of these achieve better academic performance than their peers. Three-quarters of students who take the GED pass the exam.

Missouri's DYS was awarded $100,000 for its future work. The Annie E. Casey Foundation is a private organization whose mission is "to foster public policies, human-service reforms, and community supports that more effectively meet the needs of today's vulnerable children and families."

gain relevant experience in activities like volunteer work with at-risk youth or a summer job as a camp counselor. Newly hired probation officers generally receive a period of on-the-job training when they begin work.

About 85 percent of probation officers work directly with offenders. About 15 percent of probation officers are involved in management and administration. These positions require previous job experience and may require higher levels of education or a degree in business or law.

CORRECTIONS OFFICER

According to del Carmen in *Juvenile Justice*, juvenile institutions are intended for "the 'worst' juvenile offenders—dangerous, chronic, and disruptive, such that only separation from society is appropriate." Nevertheless, placement in a correctional institution is intended to rehabilitate the offender. It is not a one-size-fits-all prospect, however. There are a number of different types of institutions with different goals for the inmates and, like probation, there is constant experimentation and readjustment in approaches.

The most secure type of institution is the juvenile correctional facility, which is sometimes called a state school. Most house about 150 inmates, and the average stay is between eight and twelve months.

A lieutenant issues orders to inmates at a jail in Fort Lauderdale, Florida. The facility runs a ninety-day military-style boot camp for juvenile offenders.

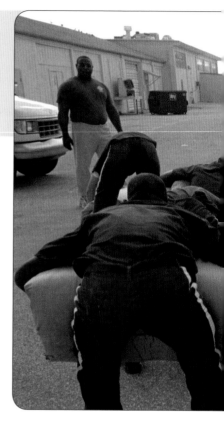

The institution provides education, vocational studies, recreational activities, counseling, and other programs. Nonetheless, the focus on rehabilitation is combined with the goals of deterring delinquency, removing the offenders from the community, and administering appropriate punishment for their actions. Juveniles with serious mental health issues may be sent to a stabilization facility, especially if they are considered to be at a high risk for suicide.

Mid-range offenders may be sent to a juvenile boot-camp program that emphasizes discipline and physical activity. The typical stay at a boot camp is six months or less. Offenders spend their days following a regimented schedule that is patterned along military lines. While in boot camp, the juveniles also receive education, job training, and counseling. Boot camps are controversial because they have not been proven to be more effective than traditional programs. There have also been cases of abuse, overly harsh treatment, and even fatalities at some juvenile camps.

Other mid-range offenders may be placed in ranches and forestry camps. At these "no-locked-doors" facilities in remote areas, young offenders take part in treatment programs and outdoor work, such as conservation projects. Each ranch or forestry camp serves about fifty inmates, and the average stay is about six or seven months.

The juvenile justice system sometimes requires that a juvenile be temporarily confined before the adjudication or at other points before beginning the terms of the disposition. Juvenile delinquents may be sent to secure detention centers, usually when they are awaiting adjudication or transfer. A delinquent that has received a disposition of commitment to an institution may first be sent to a diagnostic facility. Once there, the juvenile undergoes psychological and medical testing and, in some states, personnel at the diagnostic facility decide which institutional placement is most appropriate. Status offenders, some juvenile delinquents, and neglected or dependent children are more likely to be placed in a youth shelter. Residents at a youth shelter are restricted to the premises, but the facility is unlocked.

By law, juveniles cannot be held in adult jails unless there is a "sight and sound separation." In other words, they must be kept safely apart from adult inmates. Juveniles who have been tried and convicted in adult court, however, can be sentenced to adult prison. Depending on state law, these offenders might be held in juvenile facilities until the age of eighteen and then transferred to adult prison, held in adult prison but segregated by age, or mixed in with the general prison population. In a practice called blended sentencing, juvenile judges may impose juvenile sanctions to be followed by adult sanctions when the offender turns eighteen. In this way, judges can require longer periods of confinement for offenders whom they deem deserve harsher punishments.

The duties of corrections officers vary, depending on the setting, as do the job requirements. But a corrections officer in any institution will benefit from a background working with troubled youth. A corrections officer must be aware that he or she is a role model for the residents, and he or she must have strong communication and supervisory skills. A corrections officer will have to resolve conflicts and manage crises. He or she also has to make safety a priority. In juvenile institutions for serious and violent offenders, extreme precautions are necessary to protect the safety and well-being of the officers and juveniles alike. The job is made more difficult by overcrowding in some institutions. Everyday tasks include performing inspections,

A New York State parole officer warns young offenders held at a juvenile facility that criminal behavior could land them in adult prison later in their lives.

booking new residents into custody, and filling out paperwork. A corrections officer may be required to work night shifts or holidays.

The ideal candidate for a position in juvenile corrections should have a degree in criminal justice, social work, or a related field. But institutions will often hire candidates with a certain amount of relevant college credit or experience. Once hired, the candidate generally starts out as a trainee. He or she receives training in topics like facility operations, health issues, and juvenile rights. Once the candidate has been promoted to full juvenile corrections officer, he or she may work up the ladder to sergeant and then lieutenant.

Juvenile corrections facilities require administrators, directors, coordinators, supervisors, and other personnel involved in the institution's operation. There may be counselors, recreational therapists, teachers, tutors, and specialists in various treatment programs. Programs such as ranches and forestry camps will also include staff members like youth wilderness instructors. Institutions are held accountable by corrections internal affairs officers and correctional investigators, who ensure that policies and rules are followed and juveniles' rights and well-being are protected.

4

RELATED CAREERS IN JUVENILE JUSTICE

Job seekers who are interested in a juvenile justice career should keep in mind that there are numerous jobs available in this area that remain outside the fields of law and corrections. You don't have to be a lawyer, judge, or corrections officer to get involved in a positive way in the juvenile justice field.

During every step of the process, a juvenile encounters various professionals who are involved in different aspects of juvenile justice. A police officer or other law enforcement officer is often a juvenile's first contact with the system. A diversion specialist might arrange the details for alternate sentencing. If the case goes before a judge, then the juvenile might be assigned a court-appointed special advocate (CASA). Once the juvenile has received a disposition, he or she may work with counselors and educators. The personnel involved in a juvenile's case vary, depending on the circumstances, and practices change from one state to another.

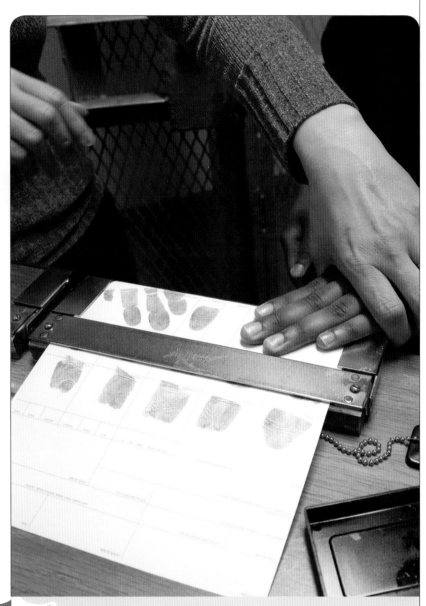

A girl has her fingerprints taken at Southern Oaks Girls School, a secure juvenile correctional facility that provides education and treatment programs for delinquent girls.

One example of a variation on the usual procedure is the juvenile drug court. Drug courts were developed as a way to intervene more efficiently and effectively in cases of teen drug use. (Drug court deals with drug users, not dealers or manufacturers.) Regular juvenile court often fails to place drug users in treatment programs quickly enough. Drug courts require the participation of family members, drug or alcohol counselors, and sometimes representatives from school and community organizations. The process is often more intensive than that of traditional juvenile court, and the judge holds frequent hearings to monitor the juvenile's progress. In some cases, drug courts are viewed as a diversion program, rather than a formal adjudication. Those interested in a career in juvenile justice could train to become a drug or alcohol counselor to help teens avoid the pitfalls of substance abuse and addiction, and to advise them should their substance abuse land them in court.

A juvenile's disposition may require that he or she participate in day treatment or evening treatment programs. These programs may be appropriate for juveniles who need strict supervision. They can also serve as an aftercare measure for juveniles who have been released from confinement. Juveniles who are not enrolled in school attend day treatment programs. They may receive counseling, life skills training, and educational support. Youths who are enrolled in school attend similar evening treatment programs. These programs require skilled, caring, and dedicated counselors who are strict but fair and compassionate. Above all, they must be committed to the well-being and reform of juvenile offenders.

LAW ENFORCEMENT OFFICER

Police officers and other law enforcement officers fight crime and keep the public safe. They enforce laws, preserve the peace, catch criminals, prevent crime, and educate the public about safety and security. They may be called upon to respond to a wide range of situations at a moment's notice. Sometimes, they will be required to deal with juveniles. These may be juvenile delinquents, status offenders, neglected or dependent children, or victims of crimes.

A police officer should be aware of state and city laws that apply to juveniles, as well as department policies. Juveniles have most of the same constitutional rights as adults, such as the right to remain silent and the right to an attorney when being taken into custody. In addition, many states require that juveniles' parents be contacted when they are detained.

The officer must have probable cause when taking a juvenile into custody. In some cases, this

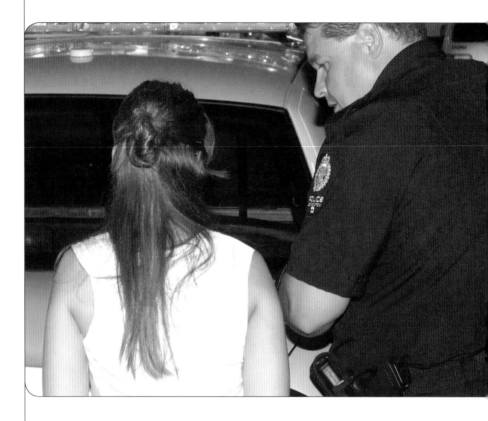

means that the officer must be reasonably certain that the suspect has committed a crime or was in the process of committing a crime. The officer may establish probable cause through reliable information or through his or her own observation and experience. Officers have a great deal of latitude for taking juveniles into custody, however. An officer may justifiably take a juvenile into custody in circumstances in which it would not be legal to detain an adult. Examples include situations in which the officer

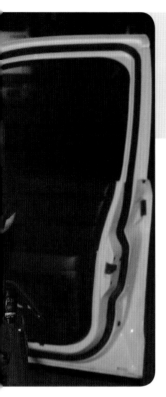

A law enforcement officer should be knowledgeable of laws and procedures pertaining to juveniles. In some states, for example, a parent or lawyer must be present at police interrogations.

believes the youth is in danger or has committed a status offense, such as running away from home.

Police also have a great deal of discretion regarding whether or not they should formally take the juvenile into custody or deal with him or her more informally instead. They base their decision on factors like the type of offense committed and whether or not the juvenile has already been involved in the juvenile justice system. If the officer chooses to deal with the situation informally, then

A New York Police Department recruit takes notes in a log as part of police academy training. Recruits learn practical skills, such as handling firearms, and also study academic subjects.

he or she is essentially giving the youth a second chance. The simplest option is just to ignore the misbehavior. Another option is to issue a warning and contact the juvenile's parents and/or probation officer. For more serious situations, the officer may take down an official statement and give an official warning. The officer may also refer the juvenile to a social services agency.

Most police officers work as patrol officers who enforce the law on their beat, or assigned area.

Some officers, called juvenile officers, specialize in dealing with juveniles and preventing delinquency. In large cities, certain police units may specialize in combating gang activity. Specialized officers receive additional education and training in juvenile justice issues and tactics.

Becoming a police officer is an intensive process that requires rigorous interviews, testing, background checks, and a medical examination. Applicants must have a high school diploma or a GED, and

69

higher levels of education generally give candidates an edge. Once a law enforcement recruit is hired, he or she must attend a police academy. Most recruits start out as patrol officers. After a couple years, they may apply for specialized positions. A job on the police force often requires that officers work nights, weekends, or holidays.

DIVERSION SPECIALIST

Minor offenders may be eligible for diversion, which is sometimes called alternative sentencing. These include first-time offenders who have committed non-serious offenses. Examples might include property damage or minor theft, though eligibility for diversion varies from one state to another.

A juvenile diversion specialist—other possible job titles include diversion officer or alternative sentencing specialist—supervises the offender's progress through the diversion program. The process begins with a meeting of the youth, his or her parents, and the diversion specialist. The diversion specialist evaluates the case and sets up an appropriate diversion program. The youth signs a formal agreement or contract that states the terms of the program. He or she completes the diversion program under the supervision of a diversion specialist. A diversion program may require community service,

Teens share their thoughts and feelings during a group therapy session. Therapy, counseling, and other programs help offenders reach the end goal of successful rehabilitation.

restitution (payment for damages or loss), counseling, educational workshops, or writing projects like an essay or a letter of apology.

The diversion specialist must thoroughly study the juvenile offender's case history before making a recommendation, and the specialist must also monitor the offender's progress as he or she completes the program. The diversion specialist may need to consult with any probation officers,

Is the Social Worker In?

Social workers provide aid and services to people in need. They work to address social problems that include poverty, discrimination, drug and alcohol abuse, and mental illness. They accomplish this by working with people directly and by developing programs and policies that support individuals, families, and communities.

In the juvenile justice system, social workers offer counseling, group therapy, and advocacy to children and teens. In some cases, their official job title is "social worker," although the exact duties of a juvenile justice social worker vary from one program to another. Oftentimes, job titles are more specific, such as caseworker, counselor, or specialist in areas like substance abuse or mental health. These positions generally require a background in social work or other relevant field.

Many universities offer bachelor's, master's, and doctoral programs in social work. Practicing social workers must be certified or licensed by the state. In general, this involves passing an exam and gaining a certain amount of professional experience.

counselors, or court personnel who are involved in the case. The job generally requires that the diversion specialist attend meetings, conduct interviews, act as a liaison, and write reports. A good candidate for a diversion specialist position should have a degree in social work, criminal justice, behavioral science, counseling, or a related field.

CARRYING OUT JUSTICE

When a youth does not have a parent or guardian, the judge may name a court-appointed special advocate (CASA) to represent his or her best interests in court. A CASA is most often involved in cases of dependency or neglect, although CASAs sometimes work on behalf of delinquents. CASAs gather information on the youth, make recommendations in reports, and arrange for the child and family (if there is one) to receive social services. Many are volunteers, though requirements for a CASA differ from one state to another. Often, CASA programs are run by staff members, which can include lawyers and social workers, as well as volunteers.

Courts may also appoint an advocate for the victim of juvenile crime. The victim advocate explains the procedures of the juvenile court and keeps the victim informed of developments in the case. If the offender goes to court, then the

advocate accompanies the victim to court hearings. The advocate helps that person file a victim impact statement, which may include a request for restitution. Usually, the victim advocate works for the prosecutor's office or for the probation department.

A parent and child, along with youth intervention workers and a probation officer, participate in a restorative justice neighborhood accountability board hearing in Gilroy, California.

One approach that is intended to help both the offender and the victim is a model called restorative justice, which is a form of conflict resolution. The parties involved or affected by the offense come to an agreement on how the offender can work to undo the harm that he or she has

Jane Addams

Jane Addams (1860–1935) was a social reformer, writer, and pacifist best known as the founder of Hull House in Chicago. In 1931, Addams became the first American woman to win the Nobel Peace Prize.

Hull House, a settlement house, provided services and resources for the poor, especially working women and their families. The founders of these kinds of houses "settled" in poor neighborhoods and tried to address the social ills around them. Hull House offered day care for children, evening classes in a variety of subjects, and many cultural opportunities. It had a community kitchen, a library, an employment bureau, and a gymnasium.

Addams and other Hull House reformers worked tirelessly for social justice and the improvement of working and living conditions for the poor. They founded the Juvenile Protective Association and a Juvenile Psychopathic Clinic, later known as the Institute for Juvenile Research. Addams's lobbying helped spur Illinois lawmakers to establish the first juvenile court.

Jane Addams has been called one of America's pioneering social workers for her advocacy of the underprivileged.

caused. Restorative justice programs are often recommended as diversion and are not formal court proceedings. Participation is voluntary for the victim. The victim should not be pressured to take part.

Restorative justice often takes the form of mediation between the offender, his or her parents or guardians, and the victim. A trained mediator assists them. The victim has a chance to describe the impact of the offense and try to understand the juvenile's motivations. The offender must directly face the real consequences of the offense. All parties come to an agreement on appropriate penalty, such as restitution or community service. It is hoped that this process allows all parties to benefit from involvement with the juvenile justice system.

TREATMENT AND EDUCATION

Whether or not an offender is dealt with formally or informally, the end goal of the juvenile justice system is generally rehabilitation. Many juvenile delinquents are required to attend counseling as part of their treatment program. Counselors may work directly for the juvenile justice system through a court or another institution. They may also work for other branches of the social welfare system or for private organizations. Typically, counselors are required to have a degree in counseling, behavioral sciences, or social work. Psychologists may be required to hold a graduate degree in psychology or counseling.

A delinquent's treatment program is tailored to his or her needs. It may include individual and group therapy, education, prevention programs, or crisis intervention. Family counseling sessions address issues in the youth's home life that contributed to his or her delinquency. Substance abuse counselors help juveniles with alcohol, tobacco, or drug problems. Youths may be required to take anger management classes. Sex offenders are generally required to complete an intensive program that addresses their attitudes and behavior patterns. Youths with mental health issues meet with mental health specialists or psychologists to deal with their issues. Delinquents who are confined to an institution may participate in programs designed by a recreational therapist.

In addition, delinquent youth often pursue educational and job training opportunities while they work their way through the juvenile justice system. Teachers employed by juvenile justice programs should have a degree in education and, in some cases, state certification. Delinquents who are not enrolled in school may participate in literacy classes, tutoring, vocational training, remedial education, GED preparatory classes, or other types of classes depending on their needs. Employment counselors may offer guidance in finding a job and making the transition to working life.

NEGLECT AND DEPENDENCY CASES

Most examinations of the juvenile justice system focus on the treatment of delinquents. Neglected and dependent youth, however, are not involved with the system due to delinquent criminal acts. Instead, they fall under the jurisdiction of the juvenile court because of the conduct of their parents or guardians. Examples of neglect include physical, emotional, and educational neglect, as well as physical, sexual, and emotional abuse. Dependent youth are those who must rely on the court because their parents are incapable of caring for them, usually because of physical or mental disability.

When there is a report of child neglect or abuse, the case is investigated by the child welfare system. Nationally, the agency responsible for child welfare is the Children's Bureau, which is part of the U.S. Department of Health and Human Services. There are also state and local agencies, such as child protective services or social services departments, which are responsible for child

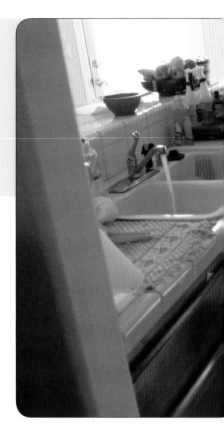

Claudia Boyd inspects the home of a couple who wish to serve as foster parents for a grandchild. A juvenile court investigator, Boyd evaluates homes of prospective foster parents for safety.

welfare. Government agencies work together with private and community organizations.

If the case meets the legal definition of dependency or neglect, then child protective services workers investigate and assess the situation. The youth is not removed from the home unless a caseworker believes he or she is in immediate danger. In most cases, dependency and neglect cases are dealt with informally. The child welfare system helps families resolve the causes of the situation. In most cases,

the ultimate goal is to keep families together or, if the child has been removed from the home, to reunite families.

If the informal options fail, or if there are special considerations, then a case of dependency or neglect goes before juvenile court. (Criminal charges, such as severe abuse, are dealt with separately in adult court.) The judge rules whether or not the evidence supports the allegations of dependency or neglect. When the allegations are found to be true, the judge hands down a disposition. The youth may be returned to his or her family. He or she may be placed in foster care, either with a relative or with a family that has been appointed by the child protective services agency. The youth's parents could lose custody.

Child protective services workers—other possible job titles include child protective services specialists, child welfare workers, or child protective investigators—have the responsibility of investigating and reviewing reports of abuse and neglect. They must have a thorough understanding of state laws and procedures concerning child protection. They must also be able to recognize symptoms of abuse.

Youth who are placed in the custody of child protective services are assigned a caseworker. If the youth is placed in foster care, then the caseworker makes sure the home is suitable. He or she may find a new placement for the youth if it becomes necessary. When the goal is reunification with the family, the caseworker arranges family visits and monitors the family's progress in fulfilling the conditions for reunification. When the goal is adoption, the caseworker helps the adoptive family with arrangements. He or she reports progress toward the youth's goal to the court. The caseworker also offers counseling to families and to the youth, and he or she acts as a liaison between the different agencies and organizations.

PREPARING FOR A JUVENILE JUSTICE CAREER

5

t's hard to describe a "typical" worker in the juvenile justice system. On the one hand, there are many professionals with advanced degrees, such as attorneys, psychologists, and policy makers. On the other, some positions, such as in corrections, may be filled by candidates with a high school degree, some college credit, and related experience. In between, there are a wealth of opportunities available to job seekers with two-year or four-year degrees. All of these people have the potential to make a crucial difference in a juvenile's life.

Just as there are many different types of careers in juvenile justice, there is great variety in workplaces and hours. Court personnel typically work nine-to-five jobs in the courthouse. Probation officers often travel extensively and sometimes work late-afternoon and evening hours. Sometimes, they remain on call in case one of their probationers gets into trouble. Corrections officers work at various kinds of

institutions, and they may work night shifts, weekends, and/or holidays. Counselors at ranches or forestry camps spend many of their working hours outdoors.

SEEKING AND LANDING A JOB

In every area of juvenile justice, a candidate must have relevant education, training, and experience for the job. A student studying criminal justice,

This is a classroom in one of six housing pods at the County of Alameda Juvenile Justice Center in San Leandro, California, which opened in 2006. The center also contains courtrooms and medical facilities.

behavioral sciences, counseling, or social work is building a good foundation for many juvenile justice jobs.

There are also many different ways that job seekers interested in juvenile justice can gain relevant experience. Many juvenile justice programs accept volunteers to work with juveniles or to help with administrative tasks. Other opportunities exist at community groups, schools, hospitals, libraries, churches, police departments, athletic associations,

Dewey G. Cornell

Whenever there is a school shooting or other high-profile incident of school violence, parents and educators across the country react with concern and sometimes panic. Dewey G. Cornell, a forensic clinical psychologist and professor of education at the University of Virginia, has extensively studied school safety and violence prevention. As director of the Virginia Youth Violence Project, Dewey helped design a model for preventing school violence. His approach, called threat assessment, outlines a series of steps that school officials take when a student makes a threat. Most threats are not serious, but there have been cases of students being suspended or expelled for idle threats. Dewey's method is intended to focus only on serious threats. Beneath every serious threat, there is an underlying cause, such as mental illness, bullying, or personal crises. These issues can be addressed before the student resorts to violence.

Dewey earned a master's degree and Ph.D. from the University of Michigan. He has written or co-written numerous publications, consulted with the FBI on an examination of school shootings, and testified in trials involving school shootings and other cases of juvenile homicide. In 2007, following tragic shooting massacres at Virginia Tech and an Amish school in Pennsylvania, Cornell testified before the U.S. House of Representatives on effective practices on preventing school violence.

and many other organizations that involve children and young adults. Volunteers may tutor students, act as mentors, plan activities, chaperone field trips, help lead workshops, or work with children in other ways. Students may take a summer job working with kids, such as a camp counselor, or complete internships related to juvenile justice.

Once a job seeker has chosen a field within juvenile justice, the next step is the job search. There are job listings in print publications, such as a newspaper's classified ads, and online. When searching online, a job seeker should look at general job listing sites (for example, Monster.com, CareerBuilder.com, Career.com, or Job.com), as well as the specific Web sites of juvenile justice programs. Most juvenile justice departments have an "Employment" section within their Web site. Some sites for professional associations—such as correctional associations—list job openings. Recent college graduates may find job leads through their school's career center.

Finally, a serious job seeker should visit possible employers and set up informational interviews. Even if they are not hiring at the time, these employers may be able to give tips about other prospective job openings in the area and offer you up-close insights into the work being done there. Informational interviews are an invaluable way to

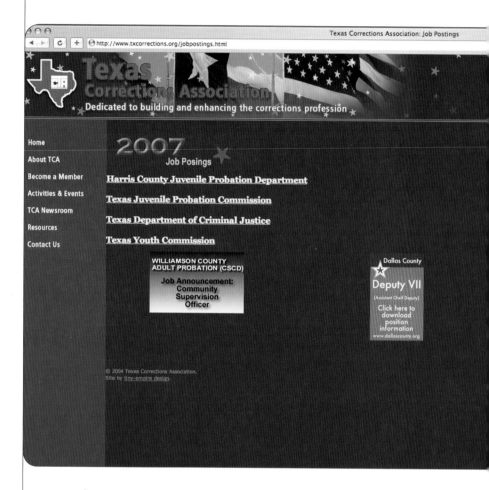

make contacts in your field of choice. The person you speak to may know someone who is hiring or may remember you six months from now when he or she is trying to fill a newly vacant position.

Most employers require that job seekers send a résumé and cover letter when applying for a position. Government departments may also require an application form. A résumé serves as an

Professional Web sites, such as this site for the Texas Corrections Association (http://www.txcorrections. org), can provide job seekers with valuable information, news, and employment prospects.

introduction to prospective employers. An effective résumé provides relevant information that demonstrates the candidate is a good fit for the job opening. On their résumé, job seekers should describe skills and experience gained from past employment, education, or activities, rather than just listing job titles. It is often a good idea for job seekers to tailor their résumé to each employer. The

A job interview is a candidate's chance to persuade the interviewer that she is the best fit for the job. In addition, it is an opportunity to learn more about the employer and workplace.

cover letter gives job seekers a chance to elaborate on the reasons why they're a great fit for the job.

Employers generally pay close attention to an applicant's employment history, but young people and recent graduates just starting out in the workplace do not have an extensive work history. When this is the case, applicants should emphasize related education and experiences that make them stand out from the rest of the candidates. Job seekers should open a résumé with their strengths, whether it's an impressive employment record or extensive volunteer work.

The next step is the job interview. There are many books and Web sites available that give interview tips. Before the interview, the candidate should research the employer and prepare a list of questions about the organization and the job. The candidate should use his or her research to demonstrate solid knowledge of the company, court, or institution during the interview. Employees who work with children are often required to undergo a background check and sometimes a drug test. Most job seekers do not land the job on their very first interview, but every interview is a learning experience that better prepares you for the next interview. With persistence, a qualified and enthusiastic candidate is sure to find a good match in the field.

School Searches

Landmark court cases involving juveniles can potentially change the daily lives of students. In 1985, a teacher sent a high school freshman to the principal's office on the suspicion that she had been smoking in the bathroom. The principal searched her purse and found marijuana and letters indicating that the girl sold marijuana. She confessed and was adjudicated delinquent.

The girl appealed the ruling on the grounds that the principal had no legal right to search her purse. The Fourth Amendment of the U.S. Constitution prohibits unreasonable searches and seizures—police and other officials cannot search private property unless there is probable cause. Eventually, the Supreme Court held that school officials do not need a warrant to conduct searches. It also ruled that reasonable suspicion, rather than probable cause, was adequate justification for a search. As a result, school officials generally have the legal right to search a student's person, belongings, and locker. Specific laws vary from one state to another.

CURRENT AND FUTURE DEBATES IN JUVENILE JUSTICE

As long as there are youths breaking the law, there will be jobs for professionals in the field of juvenile justice. Nonetheless, the juvenile justice system is constantly evolving. There will be innovative programs, new laws, changes in policy, and landmark cases that reshape the juvenile justice system. For many, such changes offer new opportunities. Experts in the field are called upon to develop and implement new treatment models. Researchers, such as sociologists and statisticians, study the effectiveness of different programs. For others, though, change is not always welcome. Promising programs can be wiped away by shifting trends in policy. Juvenile justice often falls victim to budget cuts when government money is tight. This negatively impacts a system that, in many cases, is already squeezed for resources.

The debate continues over the issue of transferring some juvenile offenders to adult criminal court, even as it becomes more common. One argument for this practice is that some crimes are so serious that the offender should be severely punished for them, regardless of age. Another argument is that a small portion of juvenile offenders cannot be rehabilitated by the juvenile

Juveniles serving time as adults in Maricopa County, Arizona, can volunteer to participate in sheriff Joe Arpaio's Juvenile Chain Gang. Arpaio boasts that he is "the toughest sheriff in America."

justice system, and thus, it would be better to devote resources to lesser offenders who could be helped. Critics of the practice point out that mandatory transfer to adult court for certain serious crimes fails to take mitigating factors of individual cases into account. Another interesting argument against transfer to adult criminal court is that when youth are tried as adults, they are not treated like adults in court. Lawyers and juries tend to take their age into account, even though juvenile judges have ruled that they are to be tried as adults.

Dealing with status offenders has always been somewhat controversial. How harshly should the juvenile justice system treat an offender whose actions would not be considered criminal if carried out by an adult? Some experts contend that status offenders tend to escalate into juvenile delinquency. Skeptics claim that behavior like truancy, liquor law violations, or running away should not be dealt with as harshly as delinquency. In most states, status offenders are treated much the same as delinquents. Usually, though, they cannot be confined in detention centers or other secure facilities.

Drug courts have proven to be an effective means of dealing with drug offenders. Some experts have proposed expanding specialty courts to deal with specific categories of offenses. One

Girls confined at the Sierra Youth Center in Sonoma County, California, are allowed to personalize their rooms—they are not called "cells"—during their three- to eight-month stay at the center.

court might hear serious crimes, another would hear lesser offenses, and yet another would hear gun charges. Restorative justice approaches have also proven promising, and it is likely that such programs will expand in the future.

A 1992 amendment to the Juvenile Justice and Delinquency Prevention Act (JJDPA) addressed criticisms over the number of minority youths in

the juvenile justice system. The makeup of the youth population in the system continues to be a concern. According to del Carmen's *Juvenile Justice*, 70 percent of confined delinquents were minorities, a much higher percentage than minority representation in the general population. A more recent concern has involved the number of female delinquents in the system. Rates of female juvenile delinquency, including serious offenses, have been increasing.

The juvenile justice system is not perfect, but it has given second chances and a world of opportunity to many at-risk and troubled youth. Every worker in the field has stories about former delinquents who one day returned as successful, law-abiding adults to thank the people who helped them through the system. There are many benefits to a career in juvenile justice. Working with other dedicated professionals and helping troubled youth transform their lives and begin to thrive are just two of the greatest rewards.

GLOSSARY

adjudication The process in which a judge rules whether the allegations of delinquent conduct are true or denied (guilty or not guilty).

allegation An accusation; specifically, a court accusation against a juvenile offender.

appeal To apply for review of a case or particular issue to a higher court.

arson The crime of intentionally setting fire to a building or other property.

bench The seat for the judge in a courtroom; also, a symbol for the office and authority of a judge.

community service Work performed by offenders as part of their sentence.

custody Legal restraint or detention; also, guardianship, such as in a child custody case.

delinquency The violation of a law by a juvenile.

discretion The power of a judge or other official to make judgments based on principles of law and fairness.

disposition The final determination in a case; the juvenile justice equivalent of a sentence.

diversion A type of informal probation in which the case is not formally processed by the juvenile court.

evidence Data presented in court as proof of facts in a case.

expungement The act of erasing or canceling out.

jurisdiction The right or power to administer justice.

probation The act of suspending an offender's sentence and allowing him or her to go free subject to certain conditions.

rebuttal The presentation of opposing evidence or arguments.

rehabilitation The restoration of an offender to a law-abiding individual.

restitution Money or services given in compensation of loss or injury.

status offense Conduct that is illegal for a juvenile but non-criminal for an adult.

testify To state or declare under oath, usually in a court of law.

waiver The act of relinquishing a right, claim, or privilege.

FOR MORE INFORMATION

Canadian Bar Association (CBA)
500-865 Carling Avenue
Ottawa, ON K1S 5S8
Canada
(613) 237-2925
Web site: http://www.cba.org
The Canadian Bar Association is an organization made up of members of Canada's legal profession.

Canadian Institute for the
    Administration of Justice (CIAJ)
Faculty of Law, University of Montreal
Pavilion Maximilien-Caron
3101 Chemin de la Tour, Room 3421
P.O. Box 6128, Station Centre Ville
Montreal, QC H3C 3J7
Canada
(514) 343-6157
Web site: http://www.ciaj-icaj.ca
The Canadian Institute for the Administration of Justice is a nonprofit organization dedicated to improving the quality of justice for all Canadians.

Council of Juvenile Correctional
   Administrators (CJCA)
170 Forbes Road, Suite 106
Braintree, MA 02184
(781) 843-2663
Web site: http://cjca.net
The Council of Juvenile Correctional Administrators
is a nonprofit organization dedicated to improving
juvenile correctional services, programs, and practices.

Juvenile Law Center (JLC)
1315 Walnut Street, 4th Floor
Philadelphia, PA 19107
(215) 625-0551
Web site: http://www.jlc.org
The Juvenile Law Center is a nonprofit legal service
devoted to advancing the rights and well-being of
children in jeopardy.

National Center for Juvenile Justice (NCJJ)
3700 South Water Street, Suite 200
Pittsburgh, PA 15203
(412) 227-6950
Web site: http://www.ncjj.org
A division of the National Council of Juvenile and
Family Court Judges, the National Center for Juvenile
Justice aims to provide effective justice for children and
their families through research and technical assistance.

Office of Juvenile Justice and Delinquency
    Prevention (OJJDP)
810 Seventh Street NW
Washington, DC 20531
(202) 307-5911
Web site: http://www.ojjdp.ncjrs.org
A component of the Office of Justice Programs, an
office within the U.S. Department of Justice, the
OJJDP provides national leadership, coordination,
and resources to prevent and respond to juvenile
delinquency and victimization.

WEB SITES

Due to the changing nature of Internet links,
Rosen Publishing has developed an online list of
Web sites related to the subject of this book. This
site is updated regularly. Please use this link to
access the list:

http://www.rosenlinks.com/ccj/juve

FOR FURTHER READING

Ackerman, Thomas H. *Federal Law Enforcement Careers: Profiles of 250 High-Powered Positions and Surefire Tactics for Getting Hired.* 2nd ed. Indianapolis, IN: JIST Works, 2006.

Baker, Barry. *Becoming a Police Officer: An Insider's Guide to a Career in Law Enforcement.* Lincoln, NE: iUniverse, Inc., 2006.

Facts On File, Inc. *Careers in Focus: Social Work.* 2nd ed. New York, NY: Ferguson, 2006.

Grimming, Rob, and Debbie J. Goodman. *Juvenile Justice: A Collection of True-Crime Cases.* Upper Saddle River, NJ: Pearson Education, Inc., 2008.

Harr, J. Scott, and Karen M. Hess. *Careers in Criminal Justice and Related Fields: From Internship to Promotion.* 5th ed. Belmont, CA: Wadsworth Publishing, 2006.

Humes, Edward. *No Matter How Loud I Shout: A Year in the Life of Juvenile Court.* New York, NY: Simon and Schuster, 1996.

Martin, Clarence Augustus. *Juvenile Justice: Process and Systems.* Los Angeles, CA: Sage Publications, Inc., 2005.

Peat, Barbara. *From College to Career: A Guide for Criminal Justice Majors*. Boston, MA: Allyn and Bacon, 2003.

Reeves, Diane Lindsey, and Don Rauf. *Career Ideas for Teens in Government and Public Service*. New York, NY: Facts On File, Inc., 2005.

Reeves, Diane Lindsey, and Gail Karlitz. *Career Ideas for Teens in Law and Public Safety*. New York, NY: Checkmark Books, 2006.

Truly, Traci. *Teen Rights (and Responsibilities): A Legal Guide for Teens and the Adults in Their Lives*. Naperville, IL: Sphinx Publications, 2005.

BIBLIOGRAPHY

Child Welfare Information Gateway. *How the Child Welfare System Works.* Washington, DC: Child Welfare Information Gateway, 2008.

Cornell, Dewey G. "Statement of Dewey G. Cornell, Ph.D., Before the U.S. House Committee on Education and Labor, U.S. House of Representatives Hearing on 'Best Practices for Making College Campuses Safe.'" May 15, 2007. Retrieved October 2008 (http://edworkforce.house.gov/testimony/051507DeweyCornelltestimony.pdf).

Corriero, Michael. *Judging Children as Children: A Proposal for a Juvenile Justice System.* Philadelphia, PA: Temple University Press, 2006.

Del Carmen, Rolando V., and Chad R. Trulson. *Juvenile Justice: The System, Process, and Law.* Belmont, CA: Thomson Wadsworth, 2006.

Echaore-McDavid, Susan. *Career Opportunities in Law Enforcement, Security, and Protective Services.* 2nd ed. New York, NY: Checkmark Books, 2006.

Ferro, Jeffrey. *Juvenile Crime.* New York, NY: Facts On File, Inc., 2003.

Greenhouse, Linda. "Supreme Court, 5–4, Forbids Execution in Juvenile Crime." *New York Times*, March 2, 2005. Retrieved October 2008 (http://www.nytimes.com/2005/03/02/politics/02scotus.html?_r=1&oref=slogin).

Kupchik, Aaron. *Judging Juveniles: Prosecuting Adolescents in Adult and Juvenile Courts*. New York, NY: New York University Press, 2006.

Lambert, Stephen, and Debra Regan. *Great Jobs for Criminal Justice Majors*. 2nd ed. New York, NY: McGraw Hill, 2007.

National Council of Juvenile and Family Court Judges. *Juvenile Delinquency Guidelines: Improving Court Practices in Juvenile Delinquency Cases*. Reno, NV: National Council of Juvenile and Family Court Judges, 2005.

Newton, Jim. "James Q. Wilson: The Power of His Written Word." *Los Angeles Times*, June 3, 2007. Retrieved October 2008 (http://www.latimes.com/news/opinion/la-op-newton3jun03,0,2931003,full.story).

Ortmeier, P. J. *Introduction to Law Enforcement and Criminal Justice*. 2nd ed. Upper Saddle River, NJ: Pearson Education, Inc., 2006.

Pepperdine University School of Public Policy. "James Q. Wilson." 2008. Retrieved October 2008 (http://publicpolicy.pepperdine.edu/academics/faculty/default.htm?faculty=james_wilson).

Stahl, Anne L., et al. *Juvenile Court Statistics, 2003–2004.* Pittsburgh, PA: National Center for Juvenile Justice, 2007.

Tanenhaus, David S. *Juvenile Justice in the Making.* New York, NY: Oxford University Press, 2004.

Vachss, Andrew. Autobiographical Essay. 2003. Retrieved October 2008 (http://www.vachss.com/vachss/ca_2003_autobio.html).

INDEX

ABOUT THE AUTHOR

Corona Brezina has written over a dozen titles for Rosen Publishing. Several of her previous books have also focused on career possibilities for young adults and social issues, including *Careers in Forensics: Medical Examiner*. She lives in Chicago.

PHOTO CREDITS

Cover, p. 1 © www.istockphoto.com/Chris Schmidt; cover (background, top) © www.istockphoto.com/Juan Estey, (background, bottom) © www.istockphoto.com/ericsphotography; p. 5 © Larry Kolvoord/The Image Works; p. 8 © www.istockphoto.com/Brandon; pp. 12–13 © David Swanson/ *Philadelphia Inquirer*/MCT/Newscom; pp. 16–17 © AP Images; p. 19 © *The Palm Beach Post*/Zuma Press; pp. 21, 66–67 Shutterstock.com; p. 23 © Scott Linnett/*San Diego Union-Tribune*/Zuma Press; pp. 26–27 © www.istockphoto.com/Tobias Ott; p. 28 © www.istockphoto.com/Nikolay Mamluke; pp. 32–33 © Shelley Gazin/The Image Works; pp. 36–37 © Bryan Patrick/*Sacramento Bee*/Zuma Press; p. 39 © Jeff Topping/Reuters/Newscom; pp. 40–41 © Laura Embry/*San Diego Union-Tribune*/Zuma Press; p. 45 © Randy Pench/*Sacramento Bee*/Zuma Press; pp. 48–49 © Anne Chadwick Williams/*Sacramento Bee*/Zuma Press; pp. 51, 80–81 © Jose M. Osorio/ *Sacramento Bee*/Zuma Press; pp. 56–57 Robert King/Newsmakers/Getty Images; p. 60 © Mike Greenlar/Syracuse Newspapers/The Images Works; p. 63 © Sarah Hoskins/Zuma Press; pp. 68–69 Mario Tama/Getty Images; p. 71 Zigy Kaluzny/Getty Images; p. 72 © www.istockphoto.com/ Christopher O Driscoll; pp. 74–75 © Meri Simon/*San Jose Mercury News*/Newscom; p. 76 Library of Congress Prints and Photographs Division; pp. 84–85 © Dan Honda/*Contra Costa Times*/Zuma Press; p. 90 © www.istockphoto.com/Sharon Dominick; p. 92 © www.istockphoto. com/Paul Hart; p. 94 © Jack Kurtz/Zuma Press; pp. 96–97 © John Burgess/*Press Democrat*/Zuma Press.

Designer: Les Kanturek; Photo Researcher: Amy Feinberg